Hope for the Hopeless

By
Vernon Bourne

Copyright © 2007

ISBN 978-0-9797319-1-4

This book is dedicated in memory of my loving mother,
to the number one woman in my life, Miko,
and to our children, Debbie, Rick, and Stan.

A special thanks to Debbie Hodges, Jean Labruno,
and Joyce C. Lock, without whose countless
hours of rewrites and editing,
this book would have never been published.

Introduction

You're invited to experience a miracle. This book tells you how the wrong choices I made in my life led me on a downward spiral that I was powerless to stop. I was on my way to hell. I might have been there already, had it not been for the prayers of my loving mother. God heard her prayers and saved me from the seemingly hopeless clutches of Satan. Thank God for a praying mother and the miracle of Grace.

I pray that this book will help you experience God's all-encompassing love and help you realize the undeniable truth that God can reach down as far as a man can go, lift him up from the gates of hell, and start him on the pathway to heaven.

The author and his mom

Contents

Chapter	Page
1. Fame	9
2. Reminiscing	11
3. Meeting My Bride	18
4. A Search for Success	22
5. Obstacles or Opportunities?	33
6. Highs and Lows	38
7. Finally Desperate	43
8. Two Steps Forward, One Step Back	51
9. Too Little, Too Late	58
10. An About Face	65
11. Miracles Still Happen	71
Epilogue	76

Chapter One
Fame

As I came to a stop in front of the club, the familiar smiling face of a valet parking attendant opened the car door and said, "Good evening, Vern. Break a leg." You could sense excitement as I entered the club; it was filled wall to wall with people, mostly couples, waiting to see what kind of a show I'd put on tonight, as every night was just a little bit different. That's one of the things that kept them coming back for more.

In my dressing room I took a quick glance at my watch. There was just enough time for a cup of coffee . . . and I heard, "Ladies and gentlemen, here he is, Mr. Vern Dean."

"Dad, Dad, wake up."

"What?"

"Dad, wake up."

It was Sunday morning, June 27, 1976, and Debbie, my thirteen-year-old daughter, was jumping up and down on the bed, overjoyed with excitement, shouting, "Dad, Dad, wake up, you're in the newspaper!"

"I know Debbie," as I rolled over, wanting her to leave me alone so I could get some more sleep. "I'm in the paper a lot, you know. The clubs advertise."

"I know, Dad. But, you're on the front page!"

Now I was awake. "Did you say front page?"

"Yes, Dad, look!"

There it was on the front page, of not only the *Atlanta Journal,* but also on the front page of the *Atlanta Constitution*! The newspapers had done an article on the moral decay in Atlanta and printed a picture of the Triangle area of the world-famous Peachtree Street. And it just so happened that the whole front of the club where I was appearing at the time was covered with a huge advertisement of me. The headline in the paper read, "Sex For Sale, you can get anything you want—for a price." I was elated! You couldn't buy publicity like that, and this didn't cost me a dime! And the headline? So what. That's what my show was all about, sex.

Here are some excerpts from a review by *Constitution* Entertainment Writer Farnum Gray.

"The club is Joker's Wild in the heart of the strip, downtown Atlanta. Most of Dean's material is in bad taste. He gets laughs by making surprising statements that infringe on topics we have been taught not to discuss in public. He talks extensively about sexual practices and bodily functions, generally using the most taboo words. Dean said he

I loved making people laugh.

was brought up in a fanatically religious church and was taught that sex and other bodily functions were dirty and wrong. His act seems to be a crusade to violate those childhood teachings.

"Most of those in his audience look as if they, too, come from straight-laced backgrounds. He had a full house the night I went, and all of the spectators appeared over 30, dressed as if for a Lawrence Welk concert. There were a number of couples, and without exception, the women laughed hysterically. He is peculiarly dedicated to his brand of bad-taste humor, and actually waxes moralistic in his defense of it. Dean, whose given name is Bourne, is married and has 'three beautiful kids.' He said he's trying to raise them to be healthily uninhibited."

CHAPTER TWO
Reminiscing

My mind was filled with vigor and wonder as life bloomed about me. The ranch in Colorado was an exciting place to grow up. There was soft velvet grass between my toes, horses and cows and chickens to watch, and acres from which to collect curiosities to fill the pockets of my coveralls. Life couldn't get any better than this.

Actually, my life just about ended there. One day, when I was about two years old, I was playing outside by myself and fell into the buried half barrel of water in the chicken pen. My brother and sister, who were supposed to be watching me, were sitting on an old bench behind the chicken house and didn't know that I was in any trouble until they saw Dad riding home for lunch. He was standing up in his stirrups, yelling and pointing and racing his horse at top speed. Fortunately, he had been close enough to see me fall into the water barrel. Before anyone else could get through the gate and across the chicken pen, Dad, still riding at breakneck speed, stopped his horse suddenly, leaped from the stirrups to the other side of the fence, and pulled me out. He turned me upside down. I had swallowed a lot of water, but lived to tell the story.

• • • • •

I have a few early memories. One spring day, I asked Mom if I could go barefoot. She said that it was too early in the spring and that I would have to wait until May came, before I could take off my shoes outside. I didn't know what my Aunt Mae had to do with it, but I was willing to wait. Fortunately, she came to visit us that day. Off came my shoes. May had come.

The next thing I knew my mother had me over her knee as I'm crying out, "Aunt Mae came, Aunt Mae came." She felt bad for years about spanking me. She thought I had disobeyed her.

• • • • •

Since my sister and brother were several years older that I was, I played by myself a lot of the time. I never minded. I was always quite creative—like the time I had a ladyfinger firecracker with an extra long wick. There must be something I could do with it. So, I saved it until I figured out what that would be. Every day, I watched as my dad would feed the chickens. When he would throw a bunch of dried corn kernels on the ground, the chickens would run over and eat it until it was all gone. I got a great idea! Retrieving the carefully kept firecracker with the long wick, I proceeded to the unsuspecting chickens. There would only be one chance to accomplish my plans. So, I took my time. First, I threw a handful of corn on the ground and watched as the chickens quickly ate it. Next, I threw just a few kernels on the ground and watched them eat that. Each time, I threw fewer kernels until I could throw one at a time. The first chicken to get to it, got the kernel. Finally, they were trained to do exactly what I needed them to do.

Lighting the firecracker, I threw it on the ground. They rushed over to it, and yes, one of them got it. The chicken picked up the firecracker and down it went. I was unaware up to that point in my life that a chicken could actually make a facial expression. There wasn't a sound, she just kinda jerked, opened her beak, and a puff of smoke came out.

• • • • •

I also went horseback riding. Dad even bought a small sized saddle just for me. Archie was a high-spirited horse who'd been trained to work with cattle. He responded to the slightest movement of the reins and could stop on a dime. I think he knew I was a kid, and took advantage of me. We'd get about a half-mile away, when he would decide he wanted to go home, and home he

I loved to go horseback riding.

would go at top speed. When he got to the barn, he didn't stop. The door wasn't high enough for a horse and rider to both go through. It was certainly an effective way to get off a horse, but I wouldn't recommend it. It didn't take me long to learn to duck.

There were several large cactus patches behind our house, and Archie knew exactly where they were. Riding at a full gallop across the pasture, just as we'd come up to one of those cactus patches, he'd slam on the brakes . . . resulting in my flying through the air and landing flat on my back. I can't tell you how humiliating it is for an eleven-year-old boy to lay face down on the kitchen table with his pants off while his mother pulls out cactus needles . . . one at a time, with a pair of tweezers. You'd think once would be enough. But, oh no, not me. A few months later and there I'd be, back on the table with my Mom and her tweezers.

• • • • •

I don't remember where I got "Billy," but he was the cutest little white kid goat that a boy could wish for. He was my best friend. He followed me everywhere. I took him up into the mountains around us and watched him climb with the greatest of ease. He would charge at me with his head down, and just before he slammed into me, he would suddenly relax and run away, going "Baa! Baa!"

A boy couldn't have a better friend than Billy.

The rest of the family was not as fond of him as I was. He did things like chew holes in the clothes on the clothesline and jump up on top of my dad's car. But I loved him. One time I heard my dad tell a visiting family who lived on a farm about 200 miles away, that they could have the goat. When they were ready to leave, I hid with Billy in the doghouse. They left without him. I figured all was well. But one day, when I came home from school, Billy wasn't there. My mother looked very sad, but she told me that they had given him to a family who was going to butcher him. I got on my bike and rode as fast as I could to the slaughterhouse. Billy wasn't there. I cried and cried. That was many years ago, but I still remember it well. Billy was an awesome pet.

• • • • •

As a teenager, I got into several scrapes. One night, my school friend, Benny, and I figured out a way to give Christmas gifts to our girlfriends. We were too young to be allowed to date. Our parents and the girls' parents would have frowned on any visits, had they known about it. So this escapade had to take place in the middle of a cold night. We planned it carefully. I waited until everyone in my family was asleep and then climbed out of my window. Since Benny wasn't sure he would wake up, he tied a clothesline around his big toe and then strung the line out the window, across the backyard, and over the gate.

With the chill winter air filling my lungs, I tugged on the rope with eager anticipation. Since there was no immediate response, I assumed he didn't feel the first signal, so I continued pulling with renewed effort. We had to go: the damsels were awaiting our gifts.

Poor Benny was in his room, wide-awake from the first tug. While he was desperately trying to remove the clothesline from his toe, I relentlessly pulled him off the bed and across the floor.

Now the plan was in motion. With the gifts clutched in our cold, trembling hands, and our frozen breath puffing by our faces, we stealthily pedaled our bikes to the girls' home.

The sisters shared a room upstairs. They were waiting for us. We threw the gifts up to them. (My gift was a fountain pen.) Filled with the thrill of success, we hurriedly pedaled home and went to bed. All was well—until the next morning.

Being guilt-ridden for receiving gifts from the rebel duo, the girls told their parents. We all attended a Christian school, so the story preceded our arrival the next day. We were in trouble! You better believe it!

• • • • •

I was usually in trouble, anyway. I had always been the class clown and loved to make people laugh, so my reputation at school was anything but good. I attended my first school election when I was a freshman in high school. Armed with a piece of paper and a pencil, I proceeded to vote. One fellow on the ballot was named Donald. He was a very dignified young man, so I voted for "Donald Duck." This was a serious meeting, and you weren't supposed to be funny. In fact, at the school I attended, you were never supposed to be funny. I hadn't realized that the ballots would be read out loud. I began to get a little nervous. I was sitting beside my brother, who knew me quite well. He said, "Did you do something stupid?" I didn't answer. He would know soon enough. Lewis, also a freshman, read the names to another student who verified that each ballot was correct and then put it in his basket. About halfway through this uncomfortable ordeal, Lewis looked at a ballot and with a grin said, "Donald." Then, the other student looked at it with a grin and agreed. Whew! I could relax now. The rest of the reading went without incident until they got to the last ballot. Lewis picked it up, and unfolding it, he blurted out, "Donald Duck!" and then snorted, resulting in blowing both sides of his nostrils right down his face. He covered his nose with his hand and headed down the center aisle of the church with this huge long string of stuff swinging back and forth from his hand.

• • • • •

It didn't take long for my reputation as a rebel to haunt my every move. I was on everybody's black list. With no one interested in helping me, and everybody at church and school wanting to get rid of me, I was destined for further trouble.

I grew up in a church that was extremely legalistic. The leaders of the church controlled the lives of all who attended. They dictated nineteenth century dress codes and had no qualms about separating families and friends. Their church handbook was of far more importance than the Bible. They controlled the school and our parents. Any student, who was in trouble anywhere, was in trouble in the home, in the school, and in the church. Since my entire life was lived within the confined society of the church, my life was miserable.

I was well aware, from the church teachings, that leaving the church was to go to hell. The sad thing about all this was that no one in the church would help students or anyone else, for that matter, if the leaders considered the person to be rebellious. They simply expelled them from the church. There was no forgiveness from them, and they assured you, that outside of **THE** church, there was no forgiveness from God.

When I was about 15 years old, a preacher ordered me out of church. Since my family happened to be out of town, I was sitting with another boy whose reputation equaled mine. We weren't causing any trouble. I guess the preacher just decided I was hopeless. Now, suddenly, I had just been kicked out of the only church I had ever known. I knew now that I was going to hell, so I decided that to hell I would go. It didn't matter what I did now. I was already doomed.

I ran away from home, but my folks allowed me to move back. After that, my life was never the same. Outside the confines of the church, I didn't know right from wrong. Violating my super-sensitive conscience became a daily activity. I was now under no one's authority. The decisions I made were nearly all wrong.

It was God's mercy that led me in the direction I was to go next. It certainly wasn't by my wisdom.

Chapter Three

Meeting My Bride

"Imitation General," starring Glen Ford, was an action-packed war hero flick about a general and his driver. The general had a reputation, among the troops, of being brave and an excellent combat leader. At a time in World War II when fighting was heavy, the general was killed. Glen Ford (who played the part of the driver), knowing that the general's moral support and leadership were badly needed in order to win the battle, took the stars off the dead general's uniform and put them on his, then went to the front lines. Through his fearless efforts and against all odds, they won the battle and emerged victoriously over the enemy. I was so impressed with this movie that I joined the Army. Ironically, I did end up being a general's driver.

Vern with his father and mother

Stationed in Okinawa, a beautiful tropical island just south of Japan, I would meet a precious jewel that would shine in my life (even to this day). It was a warm, typical October day as I was walking in Futenma, a small village near the base where I was stationed. Then I saw her. There, within the displays of colorful sugared sweets, was this beautiful girl with long black hair and a smile that beamed. The first thing that went through my mind was, "I'm going to marry that girl!"

My precious jewel, Miko

I boldly approached Miko and asked, "Anno nay Nason, Nanji desk ka?" (Excuse me. What time is it?) She sweetly answered, "Ichi jee jugo fun sugi des." (Fifteen after one.) "Arrigato," was my reply, even though I had no idea what she had said. I managed to convince her to come with me to see a movie.

We went to the Grand Ole Plaza movie theater, where they showed American movies with Japanese subtitles. For the mere price of fifteen cents apiece, we saw a drama (starring Tony Curtis and Sidney Poitier) while I sipped a five-cent Coke and she had a Fanta Orange.

The movie must have lost something with the subtitles. There was a scene where Tony and Sidney (who were escaped convicts, handcuffed together) had fallen into a deep muddy pit and were trying desperately to get out. The bloodhounds were getting close and danger was intense. As one of them would almost make it out, the other would slip and pull them both tumbling back into the mud. It was a riveting scene. While I was on the edge of my seat, Miko couldn't contain her laughter.

Vern waiting for the general

I enjoyed being the general's chauffeur; it was a special assignment that got me out of many inspections and formations.

The military tried to discourage us from getting married overseas, making it as difficult as they could. It took us eleven months of paperwork, but on November 23, 1960, we became husband and wife.

The tour of duty in Okinawa at that time was eighteen months. However, due to the length of time it took us to get married, and also because I liked it there so much, the army allowed me to remain for two and a half years.

Having something to do was never a problem on this subtropical island, with its beautiful beaches, coral reefs, and crystal-clear blue waters. It was also the home of some of the best martial arts instructors in the world, where I studied karate for nearly two years. This did a lot for my self-confidence.

The majority of Okinawan people worship their ancestors as their guardian gods. The elders and the women of the household

Vern and Miko at the beach.

perform various rituals using incense, rice, water, salt, and green tea. Miko never did believe in this religion. I took her to a couple of different churches while we were still on Okinawa. I felt God tugging at my heart when an invitation was given, but shrugged it off. After all, I'd been taught all other churches were wrong.

Chuko—my karate teacher

CHAPTER FOUR
A Search for Success

Arriving back in the United States with my new wife, I enjoyed sharing with her a land bigger and more beautiful than she'd ever imagined.

Mom and Dad welcomed her into the family with open arms and helped us get a house in Colorado Springs. Dad helped me start a little cement-finishing business, where I would put in patios and sidewalks. The business did quite well until the winter months arrived. It didn't just slack off; it came to a screeching halt.

Buying a set of drums, I got together with a couple of musicians I had known before going into the service, and we started practicing. We ended up working a couple of clubs around town before we broke up, as they had religious scruples about working in nightclubs.

Later, I landed a job playing drums with a country band in a place called The Las Vegas Club, right across the street from where my dad was the foreman of a concrete plant. It was here that I was first introduced to "amphetamines," bet-

I started playing drums with a country band.

ter known as speed. The lead singer was passing these pills out to the band, who seemed happy to be getting them. It didn't seem like a big deal to me, so I tried one.

Not sleeping for the next two nights, I really liked this stuff! I could have mowed the lawn with scissors at three o'clock in the morning, and man, could I play the drums! In fact, the whole band could play better. Sleep was something I only needed three or four nights a week. From then on, I pretty much took speed daily . . . for the next nineteen years.

We needed a steel guitar player for our band. Someone knew this guy named Whit Taylor who lived in a motel. Apparently, he had been living there for a while, as his room was full of thousands of Marvel comic books. He joined the band, and I became his transportation (as he was a terrible driver and his driver's license had been revoked).

One night, a tall, good-looking man entered the club—dressed real fancy. His name was Bill Goodwin. Behind his brand-new Cadillac was a trailer, with "Grand Ole Opera Star" painted all over it. He had a hit record out on the country charts called "Shoes of a Fool." He offered Whit Taylor and me a job on the road, for ninety dollars a week. Wow! I finally made it to the big time.

We packed our clothes and instruments, along with Whit Taylor and Miko (who was seven months pregnant), and headed for Grand Forks, North Dakota.

The excitement of my first road job and thinking I had struck it rich didn't last long. I soon found out that I had to pay for my own gas and motel. Then, to top that off, a man from the Musicians' Union came around and informed me that I had to join the union in order to play at all!

Still undaunted, after only one week in Grand Forks, we were told our next job was in Farmington, New Mexico. We arrived in Farmington just about broke, and checked into the motel . . . where we were to meet. Nobody showed up!

We were out of money, and the only food we had was a jar of chunky peanut butter (which we lived off of for a week). The owner of the motel finally gave us some credit at the restaurant, so we didn't starve. That's where we were and what we were doing when President Kennedy was assassinated.

Three weeks later, the rest of the band showed up. Again, the job was for only one week. Miko and I, along with Whit Taylor, ended up going to Cortez, Colorado . . . where we played in a club for the next two months.

This is where our beautiful nine-pound, six-ounce black-haired baby daughter, Debbie Ellen, was born!

I took Miko and our new baby back to Colorado Springs. Then Whit Taylor and I went back on the road with Judy Kay and the Kadets. I hated leaving them behind, but I needed the work. We toured all over the South doing one-week and one-night stands; ending up in a club in Colorado Springs, where I was happily reunited with my little family.

Now, Miko, little Debbie, and of course Whit Taylor, and I were back on the road. Together again, we were heading north . . . to our next job. I was driving in front, with Judy Kay and the rest of the band following close behind us. We came over the top of a hill, going ninety miles an hour, when suddenly I realized the road was solid ice! I just kept the car steady and, amazingly, made it to the bottom of the hill safely. Staring into the rearview minor, I watched in horror as Judy Kay's car and trailer (which was filled with thousands of dollars' worth of instruments) flip end over end. Then it rolled, two or three times, down the median and finally came to rest on its top.

We rushed back to see scattered remains of the instruments and trailer. Their car had landed on its top. I saw what appeared to be Judy's crushed head sticking out from under the smashed car, with blood all over it.

I said, "Oh, my God."

Someone standing next to me said, "Yeah."

I glanced up, only to discover Judy and her piano player standing next to me with hardly a scratch on them. What appeared to be a crushed head was one of Judy's wigs on a Styrofoam head with antifreeze all over it.

**Jerry Dykes and the Western Ramblers
(That's me on the right)**

After weeks of getting reorganized, and months of entertaining at various clubs, we ended up at Al' State Line Club on the border of New Mexico and Texas (just outside of Hobs, New Mexico). We stayed for nearly a year. It was nice seeing Whit Taylor, who came by to visit us while on his way to another job. His driver's license had finally been reinstated. He was killed shortly after that in a car accident.

Since the house we lived in was right next door to the club and across the street from the state line weigh station, I got the crazy idea to open a coffee shop. Putting a counter and a small grill in the kitchen, with tables, chairs, and a jukebox in the living room, I had a sign that simply said COFFEE SHOP painted on the front, and opened for business. Our business hours began at 1:00 a.m. (after the club closed), and we stayed open until the customers were gone. The clubs weren't allowed to open on Sundays, so we were open then, too . . . selling coffee, steaks, and hamburgers.

About three hundred yards down the road from us was another club called Snuffy Smith's. His business hadn't been

The coffee shop was next door to the club.

doing very well as of late, and, well, there was a fire that pretty much closed down the business for good.

A couple of weeks later, about three o'clock in the morning, Snuffy was sitting at the counter in our coffee shop . . . drinking coffee and talking.

He said, "Ya know, there sure is a lot of liquor over there in that club. There's nothing wrong with it. It's just covered with smoke. And not only that, the walk-in cooler is full of perfectly good beer. The smoke didn't even get to it."

I responded, "Is that a fact?"

Then, he said, "Ya know, there's a law in New Mexico that states that any liquor that's been in a fire must be destroyed."

I answered, "That sure seems like a waste."

Then, he said, "The liquor authorities will be there in the morning to destroy all that liquor and beer. I'll bet if they show up tomorrow and it's all gone, they won't even report it. It'll save 'em a lot of time and work."

He finished his coffee, walked over and opened the door to leave, turned, and with a slight smile said, "You'd better hurry. It'll be light in about two hours."

The first thing I did was wake up Darryl, the steel guitar player that lived next door. We ran over to Snuffy Smith's and started hauling booze. There wasn't enough time to take it to the coffee shop so we put it in the pump house, out behind the club, and got back home just as it was getting light. The next night, we went back and moved it all over to our coffee shop.

We were in the perfect location to have all this booze. I'd play drums in the club every night until it closed. Then Miko and I would sell liquor, beer, and steaks . . . while the customers (who weren't ready to quit partying) would dance to the jukebox until they were ready to go home. We kept doing this until we'd sold all the beer and only had a couple of bottles of liquor left.

By now, I was starting to buy beer to stay in business. It was on a Saturday night, about two o'clock in the morning, when one of the waitresses (who was still cleaning up next door, in the club) came running over shouting, "The cops are on the way!" Fortunately for me, she dated a deputy sheriff.

I cleared everybody out, threw the few bottles of liquor that were left out into a field behind the house, unplugged the jukebox, took off my boots and shirt, messed my hair up to make it look like I'd been sleeping, turned off the lights, and locked the door just as several sheriff cars came flying into the parking lot. Then, I waited a few seconds after they knocked before opening the door.

He said, "We heard you had a party going on out here."

I responded, "No, sir. This is our home," as he stood there looking at the jukebox.

"Do you always have a jukebox in the living room?" he asked.

"Sir, I just like a lot of music," I replied.

He said, "You're not going to open again, are you?"

I answered, "No, sir. That's it. We've closed for good." I invited them in for coffee, but they declined my offer.

Several weeks later, while I was on stage playing the drums, Amos (a black man that made and sold hot tamales in the club) came running up to the stage and shouted to me, "A man just went into your house!"

Miko had been asleep while Debbie (who was eighteen months old) was asleep in her crib in the same room. Miko awoke to find someone trying to get into bed with her and thought, for a minute, it was me . . . as I always came home on my breaks. Realizing it wasn't me, she jumped up and began yelling, "What are you doing? Get out of here! My husband is going to be here any minute. Get out of here!" He ran out of the house and hid in his car.

As soon as Amos told me a man had been in my house, I leaped over the railing that went around the stage, ran through the club, and out the back door.

I asked Amos, "Where is he?"

He answered, "I don't know," but pointed to a man standing there and said, "This is his friend."

I asked the man, "Where is he?"

He responded, "I don't know."

After grabbing a handful of his shirt and ripping it halfway off of his chest, I screamed in his face, "Where is he!?!"

"In that car, right there," he replied, as he pointed it out.

Running over to the car, out in the parking lot, I yanked the door open. There, squatting down in the front seat of the car was this man. He looked to be about twenty-five years old, with red hair, glasses, and a flat top.

I was enraged, and my adrenaline had kicked into high gear. I grabbed and pulled him out of the car. All that karate that I'd studied on Okinawa for self-defense went into automatic. I have never been a violent man, but knowing what he had tried to do to my Miko (with little Debbie asleep in the room) was more than I could handle. I viciously tore into him, removing some teeth and breaking some ribs.

The bouncer pulled me off of him, saying, "Don't kill him, Vern."

"I'll kill you if I ever see you again," I shouted, as his friend drove him from the parking lot. They turned around and drove right back in, just long enough for his friend to reach out and grab the glasses off the ground that I had knocked off of his face. Then they sped off down the highway.

The following night, once again on stage playing the drums, I saw this perfectly healthy man (without a scratch on him) walk into the club and sit down in a booth not far from the stage. He was about twenty-five years old, had red hair, a flat top, and wore glasses.

I could feel my heart beating in my chest, as a certain amount of fear started to grip me. If he were able to walk into the club looking totally healthy after what I did to him, I was in trouble. By this time, I was saying to myself, "No way! It's not him. It can't be him."

I just about had myself convinced it wasn't, when Darryl (the steel guitar player) turned around between songs and said, "Hey, Vern. Isn't that the guy you beat up last night?"

"I don't know," I replied, "it sure does look like him."

Jerry Dykes, the bandleader and front man, was thinking the same thing and joined in the quiet conversation. "What are you going to do?" he asked. "It's break time."

I left the stage and walked directly over to this man. He looked up as if to say, "What?"

Whew! It wasn't him. What were the chances that someone (who looked that much like the man I had half-killed the night before) would come walking into the same place the very next night?

The following evening, a deputy sheriff informed me that the man I'd fought with was in a body cast (with six broken ribs). He didn't mention how much dental work he would need.

One night a friend came over, late after work. He had a movie projector and a black and white silent film of a couple having sex. It was explicit and hard core. This was my second major encounter with pornography. He left the film and the projector with me for several days. I watched it over and over. I didn't think of it as something bad, but that it was just awesome that they had the guts to do it on film. I knew I liked watching it and that I wanted more. I started buying occasional magazines; however, they were mild compared to what is available now.

On the road again, we were in Washington State playing in the lounge at the Aberdeen Hotel where we stayed in a room upstairs. Miko was full term with our second child. The contractions were far apart and Miko was at ease, so I went downstairs and did my first show, then ran back upstairs on my break to see if she was ready to go to the hospital.

"No, not yet. Go back to work," she insisted.

I went back to work and did another show, then ran back upstairs only to hear, "No, not yet. Go back to work."

At the end of the last show, running upstairs, I said, "Okay, let's go to the hospital."

Miko resisted, saying, "No, I'm tired, I just want to sleep."

I bellowed, "Now!" I loaded her into our travel-worn car and sped to the hospital.

The doctor said, "You can see her as soon as we get her ready."

Five minutes later the nurse came out exclaiming, "Congratulations! It's a boy!"

Richard Allen was one week old when we continued on to the next job. I soon tired of working for others, so I hired a piano player and we started booking as a musical-comedy duo. We continued traveling all over, entertaining in at least twenty-six different states, including Alaska.

While traveling in the northern states (like Montana and North Dakota) we miraculously made it through

We started working as a comedy duo (that's me on the right)

We miraculously made it through countless blizzards and storms.

countless blizzards and storms, driving, at times, for hundreds of miles at ten or fifteen miles an hour with zero visibility.

A year and four months after Ricky was born, we were in Rochester, Minnesota. Miko was six months along with our third child. Unexpectedly, our son Stanley Earl came into the world three months early! He was born at the famous Mayo Clinic. The doctors gave us little hope for his survival. They told us if he did make it, his chances of having brain damage were high. Our little Stanley spent six weeks in an incubator, and one week more at the hospital. Miraculously we brought home a healthy son. Praise the Lord!

I believe it was my mother's never-ending prayers for me and my family that led God to keep and protect us so many times. Yet despite this, I was very bitter about the church and steadily grew further and further from God.

Mom and Dad still attended the same church in Colorado Springs. Years later, I would learn that it was a cult. They somehow convinced my sweet mother that it was necessary to disown me, so my mother sent me a letter, that was terribly painful for

Debbie and Ricky on the steps of our new home

her to write, telling me they never wanted to hear from me again. Don't write, don't call, don't come and visit.

I found a place in the country by a small stream, sat down, and just cried.

By this time, we were sick of musty motels and started pulling a travel trailer from job to job. At least it gave us more of a sense of home. I had a week between jobs so we drove to Lake Melacka, Minnesota for a fishing vacation. The kids all had bad colds, so I went fishing alone for the next few days. Lake Melacka is a fairly large lake, big enough so that if you're in the middle of it, you cannot see the shoreline. At least, I couldn't this one particular night.

My concept of God was warped and getting worse. I believed He was some kind of monster, insidiously waiting, watching for me to make a mistake. All my past influences were now being rationalized. It was overcast so there were no stars. I was far enough from shore that there were no lights. Sitting in that boat, in total darkness, with the sound of the water lapping against the side of that little boat . . . I started talking to God.

CHAPTER FIVE

Obstacles or Opportunities?

As I started talking to God (out there that night on the boat)—not listening, just talking—I said, "What kind of a God are You, anyway!?! I didn't ask to be born! And now, You're telling me that if I can't find the true religion out of hundreds of religions, You're gonna send me to hell . . .where I'm gonna burn in fire and brimstone for eternity!?!"

I cursed God and shouted obscenities at Him, saying, "If You're really there, go ahead and get me. Here I am!" Nothing happened. I just laughed, pretty much convinced that there was no God.

We continued traveling all over the United States, from fifty-below-zero weather in Minot, North Dakota, to Biloxi, Mississippi (just in time for Hurricane Camille). By now, Debbie

My family and I on the road

We were a happy family.

was getting almost old enough to go to school, and we were looking for a place to settle down.

On our way to Chamblee, Georgia (a town about twenty minutes from Atlanta), we pulled the travel trailer. Miko, Ricky, and Stanley were in the back of the car sleeping, while Debbie was up front with me. We were cruising along the four-lane highway at about eighty m.p.h. and going down a hill (probably a good mile long). No other cars were in sight, and I was playing around and having fun with Debbie. When I reached to tickle her, I somehow jerked the car . . . just enough so that the trailer started to whip.

Going much too fast now, the trailer was radically swinging from side to side, actually riding on two wheels. I knew if I didn't do something drastic, we were going to die. Since there were no cars on the road, I was able to swerve the car across all four lanes of highway (managing to set the trailer back on all fours again).

A year or so earlier, Miko had became part of my act, doing Hawaiian and Tahitian dances. Scheduled for a two- or three-week engagement, we were a big hit at the North East Club, so they kept us on for three or four months. From there, we booked into the Velvet Swing Lounge in downtown Atlanta. Having stayed there for several months, we then went right back to the North East Club for another extended engagement.

Miko joined the act, doing Hawaiian dances and playing cocktail drums.

Trading our travel trailer in on a brand new twelve-by-seventy-foot mobile home, we were able to enroll Debbie in school. We had found a home!

It was in the late sixties, hippies and drugs were prevalent, and people were tired of the war in Vietnam.

Up to this point in my life, the only drugs I used were amphetamines, though I took them daily. Of course, alcohol was a given, which I drank nightly. But now I'd been hearing so much about marijuana that I wanted to try it out. Walking downtown, on what was referred to as "The Strip" (where all the hippies hung out), I purchased one joint of marijuana.

It made me high, all right. It also made me unable to remember my lines. But I really didn't care that much as every-

By now, I was working at the Follies in Atlanta.

thing was funny . . . to me! The short-term memory loss was barely a bother. Smoking more and more, I also discovered a whole new group of friends, with only one thing in common: we smoked pot.

By now, working at the Follies in downtown Atlanta, I was doing stand-up comedy. I'd do one or two twenty-minute shows at lunchtime and then two or three twenty-minute shows at night.

Getting to be quite popular in and around Atlanta, I found a nightclub for lease and opened my own club, The Purple Onion. Business was getting good. Then, inevitably, this man wanted to see me one night after we closed. As we conversed in one of the booths, he told me how we were going to make a lot of money through gambling and prostitution. My response was that I wasn't interested, as I was making a go of it running a legal club.

He looked me straight in the eye and said, "Let me put it to you this way. Would you rather have three or four thousand extra dollars a week, or would you rather have six bullet holes in your head?"

Looking straight back at him, eye to eye, I said, "Look. After the first bullet, I couldn't give a rat's behind about the next five." Then I got up and walked off.

While looking at Miko, who was still sitting there, he said, "You know, your husband's either the bravest man I've ever met, or the stupidest. I don't know which."

It was only a few weeks later that I got a call from my bartender (who lived in a hotel across the street from the club). Calling at about one-thirty on a Sunday morning, he said, "Are you sitting down?"

I answered, "Yeah. What's up?"

He continued, "You'd better get down here. The club's on fire!"

So, I was back doing shows again. But that was okay. I loved to entertain people and make them laugh. When I'd get off stage, I'd fraternize with fans. People would tell me how good I was, feeding my ego.

Are you kidding? I loved it. I'd tell 'em, "Modesty is the ability to act humble . . . when you're as great as I am."

CHAPTER SIX

Highs and Lows

Once again, performing at the Follies, I was introduced to a couple of men who looked like farmers. They said they had some grass they wanted to sell, so I met with them the following day and took a look at it. Finding that it was of poor quality, I told them I wasn't interested. They explained how they had just come back from Bogota, Colombia (having purchased quite a large amount of cocaine), and they needed to raise enough money for plane tickets home. I didn't know anything about coke and neither did they.

At that time, you could get an ounce of pure (92%) coke for about seventeen hundred dollars. They didn't have any scales, and I only had three hundred dollars on me. I told them I would take a look at it. Driving to the bus station, one of them went in, picked up an overnight bag from a

Atlanta Nightlife
Where The Action Is
April 19, 1976

a rental locker, and brought it back to the car. Reaching in and scooping out several handfuls of this white powder, he put it in a baggy. Then I handed him three hundred dollars for it.

Not knowing how to use it, or what to do with it, I took it home, put it in the kitchen cupboard, and just left it there for some time. After inquiring around, I found there were two basic ways of using it. One way was to sniff it up the nose, and the other was to shoot it intravenously. I tried "tooting," as it's called. It tasted good, but I didn't really feel anything special.

One of the dancers at The Copy Cat, where I was doing stand-up comedy, told me she shot up speed all the time. I thought about all that coke I had and how she was shooting up amphetamines, yet she seemed healthy enough to me. I made up my mind to try it.

The minute it was in me, I could taste it from the inside of my tongue. There was an intense rush of pure pleasure that surged through my entire body. Everything had a high-pitched whispering sound, and the feeling was one of complete euphoria. Fantastic! Absolutely fantastic! I'd found the ultimate high. It was even better than sex. I was trying to convince myself you couldn't get hooked on it. I remember laughing, saying, "So what if it is addictive? I've got plenty of it!"

At first, I'd only use coke two or three times a day (whenever I was alone, or after I got off work), but then I began craving it much more often than that. Taking some to work with me, I'd either drive somewhere (between shows) and park (where I hoped no one would see me), or go downstairs in the basement of the club. From then on, shooting up (injecting it directly into the blood stream) was the only way I'd use it.

There is another method of using coke which is almost as bad, and that's called "free basing, or crack."

Becoming aware that I had developed a strong dependency on coke and was using it more and more, I finally told Miko that I had a problem. We decided I could whip it, with her help.

My brother Erwin, on the left, was down from Alaska.

That idea wasn't a solution at all. It only caused me to sneak around more. Now I had to hide, go driving, or anything to get alone so I could use it.

My brother was down from Alaska. It had been years since I'd seen him or my sister. Deciding this was the answer, I flew him further down to Georgia, where we spent a few days together. It was good to see him. Of course, I slowed way down on coke while he was there. However, I still used it several times a day. In deciding to fly up to New Jersey with him, to visit our sister and her husband, I thought it would be the perfect way to get away from coke completely.

It was great to be with my brother and sister after all those years, but they had no way of knowing I was desperately needing some coke. My brother, being a diabetic, left a hypodermic needle lying on the dresser. It was staring at me. By then, I knew I had to get back to Georgia. I insisted that they take me to the airport that afternoon; I had to come home.

I ended up selling some of the original three ounces of coke, but I still used much more than I sold. Shooting enough to get hooked, I got hooked real good.

Miko and I had a problem, but she didn't know what to do about it. I would simply lie myself out of most situations. At other times, I could convince her I was okay. It finally had to happen, though. I ran out of coke. All havoc broke loose.

Miko was at work, while I was home alone with the kids. Locked in the bedroom, I was going crazy. I had to have something. There were other drugs there, but no cocaine. In starting to shoot up everything I could find (Acid [LSD], PCP, better known as angel dust), I started getting real sick. Debbie phoned Miko at work, so Miko rushed home to take me to the emergency ward.

My arms were all black and blue from so many holes poked in them. I was deathly sick; I've never felt so ill in my life. They ran glucose into my veins (two quarts, I believe) until I started feeling better. The police arrived, but Miko convinced them that I had no more drugs at home and was going to be okay.

We wanted to buy a home and get out of the trailer. I figured this would straighten me out . . . if I had a nice house and yard. We found a big, lovely ranch house that was set back in the woods, and fell in love with it. By the time we got the financing completed, they had finished building the house. We sold our trailer for a good price and were ready to move in three days before the bank had made its final approval. Having already rented a truck to

Our ranch house, set back in the woods

store all of our furniture and belongings, we arranged everything so that the last piece to load would be the bed. That way we could sleep in the truck until we could move into the house. The owner of the house let us park the truck in our new driveway, so we could plug into the electricity and have lights.

That night one of the girls at work gave me some real good strong crystal amphetamine. I talked Miko into letting me shoot her up with this speed so she'd know how it felt. As the kids were at the babysitter's, we were alone in the back of the truck.

I loaded up the hypo, not thinking about Miko's being a lot smaller. When I shot it into her she immediately doubled over, letting out two or three choking coughs, and then passed out.

Panicked, I first threw water on Miko (which did no good at all). Suddenly I realized that she wasn't breathing and immediately tried to give her mouth-to-mouth resuscitation, but it didn't work! (I realized later that I forgot to hold her nose.)

Frantic now, I turned Miko's limp, lifeless body over on her stomach. Pushing down with both hands on her back, I then pulled up on her arms. Push, then pull. Push, then pull. As air was forced in and out of her lungs, Miko moved and coughed a little. Thank God. She was breathing again on her own. I almost killed my wife that night.

Finally we had our new home. This turned out to be good therapy: working on the yard, putting in a barbecue, planting grass, and cutting down trees. We partied a lot and used a lot of other drugs, but stayed away from coke.

I got to be friends with a guy who came to see my shows a lot. As we hit it off, he spent a lot of time at our place. In talking about cocaine, before I knew it, I was telling him how much money we could make and also how great this stuff was. When thinking or talking about coke, you never think of the bad things, only that incredible high. Knowing how to get in touch with one of the men who had all that coke, I gave him a call.

As a dog returns to its vomit, so a fool repeats his folly. Proverbs 26:11

CHAPTER SEVEN
Finally Desperate

In the early seventies, cocaine was not popular, so this guy was having a lot of trouble moving it. He had a lot of pure stuff and was willing to let it go for $700 per ounce, just to get rid of it.

I said, "No problem!" We got in the car and drove to Northern Alabama, buying an ounce.

The first thing I did was shoot some up to try it out, of course. One could always find a reason for doing coke. Having sold a lot and used a lot, I then drove back to Northern Alabama to buy some more.

It wasn't long before I was really messed up again. When cocaine is introduced intravenously, it produces an immediate intense high that lasts about twenty minutes. Then comes severe depression. The only way to keep from coming down and getting depressed is, of course, to do another hit.

One of the strange things about it is that you don't think you're going to keep using it all the time. You're just going to do one or maybe two more hits, then come down. The fact is, you have no control. If you have a gram, you can't stop until it's gone. The more you have, the more you're going to use. The only reason you sell some of it is so you'll have money to buy more.

A non-stop "coke cycle" usually lasts three to four days at a time, consisting of hitting up about every thirty minutes. One never comes down during one of these cycles. It's a full time concern. Along with all the drugs was the pornography. I would literally cover my walls with pictures: vivid, hard core pictures. When you're full of cocaine, sometimes the pictures will seem alive. You don't have time to do anything else like eat, sleep, or even leave the room. You just do coke and look at porn. Now, however, the extreme pleasure has turned into a nightmare of paranoia and a vivid awareness of a spirit world that's incredibly frightening.

Now, added to the world we are accustomed to, was this dimension of evil spirits that became more and more real. Reality gradually drifted into a far-away vagueness. I began trying to catch my tormentors: in the closets, under the bed, even in the shower! I couldn't stop. This self-perpetuating insidious alkaloid had destroyed the will. It was more than an obsession: it possessed me. I belonged to it. There was nothing more important than making sure you didn't run out. The only way I could ever get sleep after being on a coke run was with some kind of downer (barbiturates, heroin, or sedatives). Preferably it would be something to knock me out. Otherwise, I would come down too far, wherein severe depression would set in. If that happened, I would do more coke and start the cycle all over again.

I was working on and off by now; work was something that just got in my way. I would sell enough coke to make money to pay bills, and then, of course, buy more coke.

Miko knew I was doing coke, but there wasn't much she could do about it. I'd get so full of the stuff that my heart would be racing and irregular. She would sit beside me (as I'd lay on the bed) and talk to me, check my pulse, calm me down, and try to get me to go to the hospital.

Several times I tried to get help by calling drug hot lines. But in the seventies, they knew next to nothing about coke and its devastating affects. Most would say it wasn't addictive and that I should just quit. How I wished I could! One time when I called a hot line, a girl answered the phone. I told her I was addicted to cocaine and that it was ruining my life. Her response was, "I never really get high on coke; what am I doing wrong?" Wow, just the help I needed.

Sometimes I didn't even trust my own family. Literally barricading myself in my room, I truly believed that someone, something, or even entire armies were out to kill me. Looking out the windows of my bedroom, I'd see all these men hiding in the bushes, darting back and forth behind trees, closing in on me. I'd even load my guns.

Having a .25 automatic and a .22 revolver, I also had plenty of ammunition. Fear would mount as they were moving in. I could hear them saying things like, "Let's get him!" "Now!" or, "Okay, move on in!" They'd be up on the roof and in the rest of the house.

Sitting in the closet for long periods of time, I'd wait for them. Then, in a moment of bravery, I'd burst from the closet, shooting live bullets through the windows, doors, and walls of my house. Then I'd go charging through the woods trying to find them. Twenty or thirty minutes of this would bring me down enough to come back into the house, only to continue my madness.

Becoming so terrified, on several occasions I'd called the police. "Prowlers," I'd say! Or, I'd tell them someone was trying to kill me.

The cops would come flying out to my house (sometimes two or three cars). There I'd be; all wild-eyed, long-haired, beard untrimmed, freaky, and looking hippie . . . with a gun in my hand. I'd try to help the cops catch these guys. I can only imagine what they thought of me or put in their reports, but they always came. It's a miracle that I didn't accidentally shoot or kill someone, especially my own family.

By now Miko was about to have a nervous breakdown. She took the children to the babysitter's, got on a plane, and flew up to Colorado Springs (where she had a Japanese girlfriend).

Getting low on money, I needed to pay bills. Driving to South Georgia, I bought the last ounce of cocaine the guy had. Bringing it back to Atlanta, I sold all but maybe a gram of it. Now I was out of coke; there were no more options. I went to the drugstore, bought some over-the-counter nerve pills, and started my descent.

The kids and I made a big "WELCOME HOME" sign for Miko, then went to the airport and picked her up. She was happy to see the kids, but understandably not too pleased with me. At least, we were together again.

Landing a job in downtown Atlanta at a hot spot called the "Joker's Wild," I did what I do best: singing, playing piano, and telling jokes: mostly telling jokes. It was a good job as far as clubs go. I worked there for two and a half years, and things went well for me then. My family grew closer, and I pretty much had my head together (considering I was still drinking, doing speed, and smoking pot).

Amphetamines are mind- and mood-altering drugs that make a person much more daring and quick-minded than he normally would be. My entire comedy act had been developed over the years while I was using speed. Without it, my act was totally different and far less effective. What I'm telling you is that without amphetamines, my act stank.

However, the continual use of pot was affecting me in a very negative way—as it made me forgetful. The combination of the speed, pot, and alcohol made it far more likely that I would be willing to use and try other drugs (as one is in such an altered state of mind). The speed makes you feel invincible, the alcohol clouds your mind, and the marijuana makes you stupid. That's not a combination that puts you in the best of positions to make good, sound decisions.

My shows got dirtier and more cynical. I was coming down hard on morals, the church, and seemingly anything that was decent. I had an X-rated record album and three eight-track tapes that I sold from stage. They were also distributed in places that would have them, like adult bookstores.

The cops warned me about some of my material, including some about them, but nobody could tell me anything. So they arrested me! Right in the middle of a show, they hauled me off to jail. This didn't stop me. No, sir. Criticizing cops and moralists even more, I was arrested three times all together. Each time, I was charged with indecent shows and obscene and abusive language.

After the job at the Joker's Wild finally ended, and due to the fact that I'd been arrested several times for my act, none of the good clubs in town would hire me. As much as I hated being away from my family, I had to go back on the road again to work. Eventually I ended up in Pompano Beach, Florida.

Now in the early eighties, coke was beginning to be popular. I bought a gram, figuring it had been a long time and I could probably handle it now. A lot of other entertainers were using it, and it seemed there was plenty around. When you've been off of the stuff for a while, you never think about the bad part of it. You only remember the incredible rush and intense high.

After the road trip ended, I found myself out of work for quite a while. In a real slump, I started to deal coke again: not a lot, but just enough to pay some bills. I was really trying to stay off the stuff; I thought I could just use it to make some money.

It wasn't long before I was back, locked in my room, shooting holes through windows, and calling the cops for protection!

While chasing demons in the attic of the house, running across the rafters, I stepped through the sheet rock. My foot and leg went right through the ceiling into my living room. I messed my leg up pretty bad; it swelled up to twice its normal size. I'd also scraped it raw, all the way down the front of my shin. There was so much coke in my system that my leg wouldn't scab. Even two weeks later, it was still wet with little shining crystals on it. Cocaine! No scab, just cocaine. And I was one of those people who had always said, "You'll never catch me sticking a needle into my arm, not me!" I used to feel sorry for some of the people I sold cocaine to, knowing how bad it can mess up your life.

There was a picture of me, when I was about 14 years old, hanging on the wall. Many a time I looked at that picture and said, "You stupid kid. You dumb, stupid kid. What did you do?"

I would hear my family, out there in the house, from where I was in the bedroom. Oh, how I wanted to join that dimension and be part of their life again. If I could only be normal: to sit down with my family and talk, watch TV, listen to music, or play games. It was so close, yet so far away. I just couldn't reach it. It's hell, a living kind of hell.

About this time, I heard that the Joker's Wild in Atlanta (where I had worked for two and a half years) was for lease. After having talked to the man, I decided to go for it. I knew the place would make money if I were there to entertain in it, as it was a good spot for me. I also needed something to straighten me out again. I got a second mortgage on the house to raise the money for the club. I think it was $10,000. But I was already in debt too much anyway. I felt such terrible guilt about not spending time with the children, being on the road so much. When I was home I was locked away in the bedroom doing drugs. I thought I'd make it up to them and put in a big in-ground pool. It was $10,000 for that, plus the club expense, but that was okay. We could make it. I just knew we could.

Vern at age 14

The deal fell through on the club. And, yes. I went to Florida to buy a lot of coke . . . as an "investment," mind you. Oh, yes. This time I was just going to make money so we'd have enough to get a better club, or pay off the loan.

I didn't get any of this done. By now I was so physically deteriorated that I was a walking death.

I received a call from the owner of the Cheetah 111, in Pompano Beach, Florida. He wanted me to come back. Not knowing if I could handle it or not, I knew I had to do something fast. What could I lose?

Having really given up on living, I accepted the fact that there was no way out. Hopelessly hooked, I might as well take the job . . . because that's where the coke was, anyway. The trip to Florida was, without a doubt, the worst decision I've ever made. Here I was in a beautiful Fleetwood Cadillac that Miko had just had repainted; my arms and legs were a sickening yellow from hepatitis. There were several thousand dollars in my pocket, and I chose to go to Florida.

I used to love my work, making people laugh, but now all I cared about was cocaine. I could do without speed, or pot, but not coke.

By the time I got across the Florida state line, my car had started to heat up. I stopped at a station to get water and gas. Not only was the car running hot, but the transmission began acting up. I lost first gear, then second gear. So here I was, driving on I-75 in low gear, with the temperature gage pegged. Pulling into a rest stop just outside of Ocala, Florida, I opened up the hood. Little had I realized that the cooling system had erupted inside the transmission, mixing all the water and the transmission fluid together. As I moved back, away from the car, it started rumbling like a volcano about to erupt. I just stood there looking in total amazement as the radiator opened up and burped the biggest glob of oil and water I had ever seen. It blew everything apart, dumping this filthy hot mess all over the rest area.

The highway patrol sent me a wrecker, which pulled me on into Ocala. A day and a half later, I left Ocala with a new transmission and a new radiator. Then tires started blowing out. Though I lost count, I had to stop several times to buy tires along the way.

Somehow I managed to keep doing my act, and a club in Pompano kept me on for several months. Though able to stay somewhat straight for a while, I gradually slipped back into the same old pattern. It felt terrible, as I began sending very little, if any, money home. Having decided to do something I had never done before, I went to my boss and told him my problem. My request was that he send my money home (to my wife) for me, just leaving me enough to live on. He was real nice about it and started doing just that. This worked for a little while, until I started going to the bartender to make nightly draws on my check (buying coke one gram at a time). Eighty dollars, now I was just paying more for it!

It was pretty much over for me; I was agnostic in my beliefs, hopelessly addicted to cocaine, and terribly bitter against the church. Many times, I had

I was able to stay somewhat straight for a while.

checked into a motel and thrown the Gideon Bible into the trash. Full of evil and obsessed with hate, I was possessed by the devil. Having bought his lies, hook, line, and sinker, only by the grace of an Almighty God am I here to tell you this incredible story.

Having tapped out my paycheck for the week, I only had enough money to buy one hit. That wasn't even enough to get me high.

There, in a motel room in Pompano Beach, Florida, broke, out of drugs, sick and tired of it all, I sensed the strong presence of demons. Lying there on my bed, I invited them to come and take me. "I've had enough; come on, what are you waiting for?" I shouted. "Come and get me. I don't care anymore!"

Then they started coming.

Chapter Eight

Two Steps Forward, One Step Back

A dark, cold, heavy oppression came over the room. I could see and feel the demons coming! Fear gripped me as I realized they were really coming!

The last time I'd talked to God, I was shouting filth at Him out on a lake. But I knew that if there really was a God, I needed Him now. It was now or never. Knowing that since there are evil spirits, there had to be good ones, I said, "Look. I don't know who You are, or what to call You, or what Your name is. Maybe it's God. I don't know, but I need help. I'm in a lot of trouble, and I can't take it anymore."

As it was two or three in the morning, I started talking and praying very softly at first, for fear that the neighbors might hear. But finally, no longer caring, I cried my heart out to God for help. "Oh God, if You're there, if You can hear me, free me from this terrible thing! Free me from this terrible power! I know for sure there are evil spirits, so there's got to be good somewhere! I've made a terrible mess of myself and my life. I'm in a lot of trouble. I don't want to die. Help me. Please, help me."

Suddenly something started to happen inside of me. There was a tug of war going on. Things were trying to hang on, and something was pulling them loose. Realizing my prayers were being heard, I cried out all the more. As I kept crying out to God, the demons were being wrenched from my body, one at a time, though they were fighting violently, trying to stay.

Then, just as suddenly, I had a vision. I was chained hand and foot to a solid concrete wall with a speeding sixteen-wheeler coming straight at me, and Satan was at the wheel. There was no possible way out; even if he had slammed on the brakes, he couldn't have stopped. I could see him laughing. Only having a moment, I cried out to God, "HELP ME!"

In an instant, from off to my right, came a large white tank. It blew that truck into a million pieces and the chains fell off.

Now the demons had no choice; there was a much greater power. They had to leave. I could hear them hopping off the bed like little bunny rabbits and leaving. They were gone!

I'M FREE! I'M FREE! THANK YOU, GOD. THANK YOU!

I fell back on the bed, totally exhausted: they were gone! There was no questioning what had just happened.

I felt hollow and completely empty, and it scared me. Now I was reaching out to God again, praying, "Oh, God. Don't leave me empty like this. They'll come back. Don't, please don't leave me empty. Fill me with something so they can't get in. Don't let them come back!"

With my arms and fingers reaching for heaven, as hard as I could, I was shouting, "Oh, God. Fill me with something. Fill me with something, so they can't come back."

It started at the top of my fingers and felt like pure, white, cold (not chilling), beautiful, pure, clean milk. It came down through my fingers, through my arms, and then surged through every crevice and the innermost parts of my body. Filling me completely, it left not so much as one hair on my head empty. I was clean and free! Beginning to laugh and cry, I rejoiced, "I'm free and clean!" Oh, what joy! I wasn't going to die. I wasn't doomed. I was free!

When I called Miko to tell her what had just happened, she sounded happy. But, after what I'd put her through, it would take a lot more than a phone call to convince her. Then I went back to my room and threw all my needles and drug paraphernalia away.

One of the most amazing and miraculous things about my newfound freedom was the way God delivered me from cocaine. Not only did I have no further desire for the drug, even just the thought of it was repulsive to me.

• • • • •

Going to work that night full of new life, I was bubbling over with joy and happiness. I couldn't wait to tell my fellow employees about my experience. They didn't know what to think of me, as I was a completely different person. For years I'd suffered from stage fright, though few people knew that. That was gone, too! There wasn't even a sign of it. My shows made remarkable improvement, as my whole personality changed from an unhappy cynic with negative thoughts, to someone vibrant, happy, and positive. I felt like a real man again, for the first time in years.

The stage fright was gone.

How well I remember going to a shopping center the next day. It was just before Christmas, and there were decorations everywhere. One of the first things I noticed was how happy everyone looked. It was a whole new fabulous world I was in. I just loved it!

Beginning to warn others about the terrible dangers of cocaine, I was the only male entertainer among forty or fifty girls (most of whom, did coke). Few of the girls ever bought it, as coke was readily handed out (folded up in money as tips) to the girls from the customers (most of whom were men). It was the easiest way to get girls. If you had coke, you could get the girls.

Flying home for a weekend, and then back to Pompano for two or three more weeks (to finish up that engagement), I talked

We all felt a wonderful love growing and drawing us together.

to as many of the girls as I could. Telling them of the great danger involved with drugs, I related my experience with God and how I was delivered.

Now back in Georgia, with my family again, I was getting closer and closer to Miko and our children. We all felt a wonderful love growing and drawing us together. Once again, working at one of the better clubs in Atlanta, I was happy to have the opportunity to keep sharing my testimony of freedom to many people. Continuing to warn people of the dangers of drugs, I'd share how I had been freed from the devil.

On the road again, in Washington, D.C., my show was doing great and my spirits were high. As I flew back to Georgia right after the D.C. engagement, my father and mother were on their way down to see us. This was a special occasion, as I hadn't seen them for many years. With such huge valleys of theological differences, everyone seemed to stay away from us. We got along great for a few days . . . at least, until we started discussing religion. They ended up going home early. We all felt bad about that.

One of the girls I worked with gave me a book called *The Prophet* by Kahlil Gibran. I ended up buying another book by the same author, entitled *Jesus, the Son of Man*. From the title, I somehow thought that this book would coincide with my beliefs that Jesus was just a man. But, even though the book has many inaccuracies, it did convince me that Jesus was the Messiah. How far I still had to go, only God knew, though, as it turned out, it was an incredibly long way.

Working in Atlanta again, I really enjoyed being with my wife and kids. Though feeling the importance of teaching them about God, I still would not accept the Bible as a legitimate source of information. Thus, my efforts were limited.

When I got an offer to go back to Washington, D.C. again, the man sitting next to me on the plane turned out to be a drug dealer on his way home (after buying a supply of coke). Yep. You guessed it . . . back on coke again.

By the time I had finished the job and returned home to Atlanta, it was obvious that I was messed up . . . again. This time Miko had her fill of me and left with Stan and Debbie, staying at a friend's house. Rick wanted to stay with me.

Now, it was just Rick and me in that big house. Everything was different with my wife and two of the children gone. I was out of coke (again), and the phone was constantly ringing. Bill collectors kept calling. Obviously, none of the bills were being paid.

After I got some sleep, Rick and I just sat around wondering what to do next. Knowing I had to do something to keep from losing the house, I began selling some of our furniture. The first item that sold was our beautiful dining room table and chairs. Next went the china closet we had waited so long to be able to afford. Our stereo, freezer, piano, on, and on . . . I sold it all. Driving to where I knew Miko, Debbie, and Stan were staying, I saw Stan playing outside. He came over to the car, where I talked him into coming home with me.

Just before Christmas, I explained to everyone that I couldn't spend any money for presents. I needed all the money I had to pay bills. Rick and Stan took it in great stride. Stanley

Last year (shown at right) was a much happier Christmas.

started making presents for himself and even wrapped up old toys and things that were already his . . . just so he could have something to open Christmas morning. Seeing this hurt me more than anyone can imagine. Additionally in withdrawal, I was terribly depressed. I wanted my wife and daughter back home. I'd loved Miko all these years. Even when I was messed up, I still loved her. I just had a monster of a problem on my back, and I couldn't deal with it.

I just had to have some coke. Spending the money on dope, I used it all! I couldn't believe it. It happened so fast. Then it was all gone. Nobody even knew I had spent the money, not even Rick or Stan. They thought I was going to pay bills with it.

A few days after Christmas, Miko had come by and picked the boys up. Giving them each $20, she took them to the store. They each bought BB guns. A couple days later, I talked Miko into coming home (if only to talk). She agreed. Miko hinted that she might even stay, if I were straightened out.

She just sat there for what seemed like hours, looking at all the empty places where our best furniture had been. Miko just sat and stared. I remember Ricky telling her how good I was doing and how I had all this money to pay bills. He looked so disappointed as I tried to lie my way out of why I was broke. The money was gone. Miko knew from experience where it had gone. At least we were all together, even if it was just a visit.

Debbie said, "Come on, Ricky. Let me give you a haircut."

He answered, "Later. I want to go play a little while first." Then he and Stan ran out the door with their new BB guns.

It was only a few minutes later that Stan came running back into the house yelling, "Dad! Dad! Come quick! Ricky's hurt real bad!"

I asked, "Where?"

He said, "Come on. He's in the woods! He got shot."

CHAPTER NINE

Too Little, Too Late

Leaping to my feet, I shot out of the house and ran into the edge of the woods. There was Ricky, rolling on the ground with blood on his hands and moaning, "Oh, my eye."

There were three or four kids standing there watching; all of them were holding BB guns. It looked like a real battle scene. Lifting Ricky into my arms, I ran as fast as I could, putting him into the car. Stanley stayed behind to take care of the house. The rest of us jumped into the car and headed for the hospital. I drove to the nearest hospital, where our family doctor met us and examined Ricky's eye. Having been punctured, it had no fluid in it. His eye looked terrible! Lacking the proper equipment, they gave him a shot for pain and sent us to another hospital. We arrived there only to be told they wouldn't admit him since we had no insurance.

We ended up at Grady Memorial Hospital in downtown Atlanta. There began the longest night of my life.

We never did receive any good news about Ricky's eye. The BB had entered the eye and stopped on the optic nerve, killing it. The BB was never removed from his eye. Instead, they removed his eye from the socket. (He has since been fitted with an artificial eye.)

Unfortunately, this didn't bring his mother and me together. Her heart was set on leaving me, and I no longer was able to reach her.

God used this time of suffering and anxiety to talk to me and convict me. Debbie had gone to church with a boyfriend, and had some kind of a religious experience. She talked to me about it when she came home that night. Somehow, this comforted me a little.

So we wouldn't lose the house before I could sell it, Mom and Dad sent fifteen hundred dollars (to help make some of my back payments). Thank God. I didn't spend that on coke!

Now that Ricky was home from the hospital, Miko was home . . . at least, some of the time.

We had sold the house, but were still living in it, as we still had six weeks or so before closing. I knew my entertaining days were over; what else could I do? The heaviest thing I'd lifted over the last twenty years was a microphone.

I went to several job interviews, and even tried out one job hanging Sheetrock. That was a laugh. After just two hours on that job, I told the guy, "Who am I kidding? Don't worry about paying me. Just take me home." The hardest physical thing I'd done in years was mow the lawn . . . and I had a riding mower! My idea of exercise was to fill the bathtub with water, pull the plug, and fight the current.

I received a phone call from one of my nephews. He'd been through Georgia a few months earlier and had stayed with us three or four days. Since then, he'd gotten married. He and his new bride both gave their lives to Christ. He asked if I'd be interested in coming down to Florida to work for him in his roofing business. It was perfect. I was ready for a change, and this was my opportunity. I bought a tent, loaded the kids into the car, and headed for Florida. Miko stayed behind to finish the closing on the house. Once that was done, I hoped to talk her into joining us.

My nephew, Darrell, and his lovely wife, Martha, lived in a small travel trailer in Jupiter. There he ran his roofing business. They moved their trailer out of a beautiful park in Jupiter, and pulled it alongside a canal in Port Saint Lucie (where we pitched our tent). After we enrolled the kids in public school, the tent was our home for the next few months.

It was cold and the ground was awfully hard, but there were no other choices. In a way, it was fun. We washed our clothes in the canal, while watching out for the alligators. There was an artesian well nearby in the woods where we could bathe. The work was hard. Sometimes I didn't know how I was going to make it.

Debbie and I drove back to Georgia to help close on the house. Together, we talked Miko into coming back to Florida with us. Oh, happy day!

This was going to be the beginning of a whole new life. Ricky, Stanley, and our new house (that I had already rented) anxiously awaited our arrival. It was exciting! I bought Debbie and Stanley new bicycles, and Ricky a brand new Honda XL125 motorcycle. Lastly, I bought Miko a Plymouth Duster that she'd had her eye on for a while. We loaded everything we owned (lock, stock, and barrel) into a Ryder truck and headed south. The reunion was beautiful. Ricky and Stanley ran from the house to greet us. It is still fresh in my mind how Ricky lifted his mother in the air and hugged her.

I continued to roof, but was making very little money, so groceries and rent money came from the surplus of selling our house in Georgia. (There just wasn't much left after paying my parents back and buying all the gifts for the family.)

Soon, the money was gone. Miko was not happy. And unknown to me at the time, she wanted to go back to Georgia. The children and I had gone to church with Darrell and Martha two or three times, but they were rather modestly dressed. It just reminded me too much of the church I was raised in.

Darrell often talked to me about God; however, I wasn't really interested. I mean, after all I did to have my family back together again . . . everything was going to be all right now.

Things were getting worse between Miko and me. I thought, "If I could just make more money." But Miko still wanted to go back to Georgia. I told her, "You might as well go. Go ahead and just leave. I can't take it anymore. I love you and I want you to stay. But, if you don't want to be here, you might as well leave." She called some friends, and they sent her the money for the trip. Receiving a five-hundred-dollar check from an insurance premium, I bought myself a car.

The day before Miko left, I got a new job selling termite control for Sears. It turned out to be a real disaster. Though that night was my birthday, I spent it in the bedroom . . . feeling sorry for myself.

Debbie entered my room and said, "Mom wants to take you out to dinner for your birthday."

I responded, "Why? Why should she want to do that? She doesn't care."

Debbie came back, again. "She really wants to, bad. Go ahead. She said she'd probably spend too much on you and wouldn't have enough money to go back to Georgia."

Boy, how I relived that moment over and over again, and with a great deal of regret. If I could have that night to live over again, how different it could have been.

I told Debbie, "Tell your mother to just leave and get it over with."

Coming home the following evening, after my first day on the new job, my heart sank. I was driving into the yard when it hit me. Miko was really gone.

It was hard. After all, we'd been married for eighteen years. Though I missed her terribly, I had the children and they kept my mind occupied.

Debbie had some friends that lived a couple of houses down from us. Their father was a supervisor at a nuclear power plant that was in construction. After we got acquainted, he ended up getting me a job at the plant as a laborer. I considered this job to be heaven-sent: it paid more than I was making before, and it was steady work.

Stanley, the youngest of the children, adjusted to the move to Florida and liked it. He and I also had grown closer, playing a lot of catch and Frisbee.

Ricky, however, didn't like Florida, hated the schools, and wanted to be back with his mom and his friends.

Three months had passed since Miko left. When school was out, Ricky made up his mind to live with his mother in Georgia.

I consented, but believe me, I did all the persuading I could to keep him with me. From the beginning, Miko and I told the children the choice was theirs to live with whomever they chose.

When Miko came down to get Ricky, she brought along Debbie's boyfriend and best girlfriend. She convinced Debbie to go back to Georgia, too. I was so upset, disappointed, and depressed that I told Stanley, "You might as well leave, too."

God knew I had to have Stanley in order to make it. Already, I had made up my mind to go buy some coke the next day. I mean, why not? My whole world was once again falling apart, and I had been trying so hard to keep it together. The thought of their leaving was just unbearable. I had been so excited about Miko coming down because I somehow thought that I could talk her into staying. But now I was about to lose two more.

The next day at work, I bought a gram of coke and used it on the way home. Spending the last night with my whole family under the same roof, together, I was wired and miserable, in the bedroom, by myself. There are no words to describe the depression I experienced that night; or even the next day . . . watching my wife and two children pack their things into a U-Haul trailer.

Deep inside, I felt I couldn't take care of Stanley, who was twelve years old at that time. I fully intended to just get as messed up on coke as I could.

I tried to tell Stanley he should go with them. He turned, looked at me, and said, "Dad, don't you think I can take care of myself?"

"I said, "Okay, son. It's gonna be you and me." If he hadn't stayed, God only knows what I would have done to myself.

They were all packed and ready to go. I was trying to be brave and not show the intense pain I was feeling throughout my entire body. Then Miko said, "Well, let's go."

I remember so clearly. The only words that would come out of my mouth were, "Oh, no." There were a few hugs and tearful kisses. Then Stanley and I stood watching as our family drove off down the road.

Just a few days later it was the Fourth of July. Stanley and I went to Jensen Beach causeway and watched fireworks (anything, to keep from going completely crazy). It was hot, and my work at the plant was hard.

The house was much too big for the two of us, so we held a yard sale. We sold just about everything we owned, and it went for around three hundred dollars. I spent the whole thing on coke.

The next few months were lonely and hard. We moved into an efficiency motel in Fort Pierce. I couldn't do much coke . . . only because I couldn't afford it. By the time the weekly rent was paid, groceries were bought, and gas was put in the car, it just about took care of my paycheck.

During the months of July through December, God was working on me. I couldn't get away from it. When I did coke, I'd get hyper, and then, depressed. The speed was beginning to make me sick. Smoking pot only made me more depressed. I couldn't get away from the conviction. I wanted God. I really did. I just didn't know if I could ever make that move to repent. It seemed like such a very hard thing to do.

Stanley began lying and stealing, giving me a lot of trouble. The motel was not a good place to raise a young boy. The people that lived there were not a good influence.

One night a man (that used to manage the motel) came over drunk. He stood in front of the motel with a gun, shooting at his wife. Fortunately for her, he was a bad shot. And unfortunately for him, she was stronger than he was. She beat him up so badly it put him in the hospital.

It was almost Christmas, and the children were on Christmas vacation. Stanley and I drove to Georgia, picked up Debbie and Ricky, and brought them back to Florida (for the holidays).

It was so great having all the children together again, even if it was just for a week or so. We got up early Christmas morning, opened presents, sang songs, and played games. It was great! My brother and his wife were in town, so we were having quite a family reunion. They invited us to go to church with them on Sunday. God was really talking to me. It was the strongest conviction I had ever felt.

Though I remember what Pastor Brown talked about that morning, I really don't think it would have made much difference . . . because God was talking to me. Wanting so badly to turn my life around, I knew God was the answer. The only thing standing between me and God was pride. How could I humble myself in front of all these people: my nephews, my nieces, my own brother, and his wife? I mean, what would everyone think? What would my own children think? Though I wanted to accept Christ into my life, I knew I didn't have the courage to step out and go forward.

Chapter Ten

An About Face

When the sermon was over, Dr. Brown asked everyone to stand. My hands hung onto the back of the seat in front of me. I just knew I couldn't let go and go forward. Then I heard the most beautiful words I've ever heard.

Dr. Brown said, "You don't have to come to the altar to get saved, you know. God can save you standing right where you are. With everyone's eyes closed and hearts lifting in prayer, is there anyone here who would like to give his heart to Christ and would signify it by lifting his hand, then slipping it down again?"

God had brought me this far. I had to make the next move myself. As I let go of the seat in front of me and lifted my hand, I could see (out of the corner of my eyes, like it was in slow motion) all three of my children raising their hands, too! We were all raising our hands!

Dr. Brown said, "I see those hands. Just repeat these words after me. 'Dear Lord, I know I'm a sinner, and I'm sorry for my sins. With Your help, I will stop doing what I know is wrong. I believe You died on the cross for my sins and rose from the grave. I open my heart's door to You, just now, and invite You to come in, as Lord and Saviour of my life. Lord, thank You for saving me. In Jesus' name, amen.'"

Then he asked for anyone who had accepted Christ to raise his hand. Once again, the four of us raised our hands.

As we left the church, Dr. Brown shook my hand and asked me, "Did you really mean it?"

Assuredly, I answered, "Yes, I did."

We all got in the car and drove over to my nephew's house for a Sunday dinner. All the way over there, no one said a word about what had happened. We were just happy.

After we had been there for a few minutes, I just had to tell someone. Walking up to my nephew's wife, Martha, I said, "Ya know? I think I just got saved."

She replied, "Boy, will Darrell be happy!"

Somebody said, "Vern, there's a phone call for you in the other room." It was my mom, calling from Alaska. What perfect timing.

"Mom, I just got saved!" My voice echoed words of pure joy through the phone (to a mother who had been praying for me for so many years).

She said, "Praise the Lord, Vernon. Praise the Lord! I can die now."

Understanding her completely, I still replied, "Well, don't." Mom and Dad were both ecstatic.

We went back to church that night. The pastor got us all up in front and introduced us. I gave a short testimony.

As we stood there, Dr. Brown asked, "Everyone here that will pray for Brother Vernon and his family, the Lord helping you to remember, would you raise your hand?"

Tears came to my eyes as I felt a surge of confidence swell within me. Seeing all those smiling, friendly Christians raise their hands, I felt that I had found a home.

The heavy burden I had carried for so many years was gone. The terrible emptiness was now filled with the love and peace of God.

I had tried and failed so many times before, but this time was really different. Now the need for drugs was gone.

It is the greatest high in the world to be founded on the Rock of Jesus Christ, our Lord, to know my sins have been washed away! It is also nice to get high on God, without getting so depressed when you come down. Getting saved was the most important step in my life. However, it was just the beginning of a total reconstruction of my entire mental thought process.

The ocean had never looked so beautiful as I drove to work the next day. Everything seemed different. It wasn't very long until everyone I worked with realized that I was a changed man. After so many years of night clubs and X-rated comedy, the renewing of my mind was a task of monumental proportions that only God could accomplish.

Dr. Brown gave me a pocket-size Gideon Bible that I kept with me all the time. I would read on my breaks and after lunch. At first I was self-conscious about what the men on the crew would think. Then God pointed out how they used His name in their conversations all the time. Why should I be ashamed to read His Word?

Once, buying a whole bunch of gospel tracts, I distributed them all over the plant. I began memorizing scripture, witnessing, and sharing my faith to anyone who would listen. Despite my blundering lack of skills in sharing my faith, I managed to convince a couple of men to visit our church. One man and his girlfriend went forward at the end of a service.

It has taken a long time, and there have been many battles to fight, but God has been with me all the way. I found the strongest weapon I have against the forces of evil is God's Word. Prayer, memorizing scripture, and meditating on God's Word have caused the devil to flee from me many times.

I mentioned earlier how I'd had problems with Stanley's lying and stealing. Over the years, I tried every approach I could think of to break him of those bad habits, but nothing ever seemed to do any good. Wouldn't you know? When Stanley got saved, he changed completely. There were a couple of times at first when he slipped and lied to me. However, he would then come to me, confess, and ask for forgiveness.

I can testify personally, without a shadow of a doubt, that it's true what the Bible says, "When a man be in Christ, he is a new creature. Old things are passed away, behold all things are become new."

Hallelujah! I'm free!!!

Debbie and Rick went back to Georgia and started attending services at a large Baptist church, while Stan and I, of course, went to the community Bible Chapel (where we'd been saved).

"What am I gonna do now?" I asked Dr. Brown.

He said, "Vern, God's going to bring your wife back to you!"

I questioned, "Do you really think so?"

"Start praying," he replied.

Pray I did! After I requested prayer at church, everyone started praying that God would bring my family back together. God let me know that I was praying for the wrong thing, that there was something far more important. Miko needed to be saved. Yes, that's it! From then on, that's what Stan, and I, and everyone at church prayed for. I also felt deep down inside that if Miko got saved she would come back to me. However, things didn't look so good. I'd call Georgia many times and talk to Rick, but his mother wouldn't talk to me.

In the meantime, God knew we needed to get out of that motel. He led us to a little 8 x 21-foot trailer. It became home for the next two years.

During this time God was helping Stan and me to grow, answering prayers and building our faith.

Loading our dirty clothes into the old Dodge, we headed for the laundromat . . . a necessary chore we managed to do as least often as absolutely possible. Only, the car died. The question now was not only why did the car stop running, but why did it have to happen on a sticky, hot Florida summer Wednesday (when we had just enough time to do laundry before heading to church)?

The words "Lord, I need Your help" were repeated numerous times. I opened the hood, removed the wing nut from the top of the air cleaner, lifted it off, and set it down on the ground next to the car. Sweat was running down my face as I stood there all bent over, looking under the hood. I kept saying to God what He already knew, "Lord, I don't have any idea what I'm looking for. You know we want to go to church tonight. If I have to call someone for help, we're not gonna make it."

It was no use. I couldn't see anything that would keep the car from running, so I picked up the air cleaner and attempted to put it back on. But God had other plans. I tried, over and over, the simple task of matching a single bolt (protruding from the carburetor) to the hole in the center of the air cleaner . . . without success.

Hot, sweating, and exasperated, I set the air cleaner back on the ground and looked once again under the hood. There it was! A small, disconnected hose was sticking out of the carburetor, with gas dripping from it. I cut the worn out end off of the hose and slipped it back in place. Then, replacing the air cleaner on the first try, I put it back on. When we were finally back in the car, the presence of God was so strong. We drove straight home (to our little trailer), got down on our knees, and thanked God.

On the Sunday Rick and Debbie were to be baptized, their mother went to church with them. Miko enjoyed the service, and thereafter attended church off and on.

One Sunday, while talking to Rick on the phone, I said, "One of these days, you're gonna tell me Mom walked down the aisle of that big ole church, and got saved."

Rick asked, "What did you say?"

Repeating myself, I said, "One of these days, you're gonna tell me that Mom walked down the aisle of that big ole church, and got saved."

Then, Rick answered, "Well, she did!"

I said, "What!"

Again, he said, "She did!"

I shouted, "Praise the Lord!"

I don't have to tell you how fantastic that made me feel. When I told the people at our church, we all rejoiced together. I thought Miko would be soon coming to join me, but as time went on, things didn't look so good.

It had been well over two years since Miko left me. Things really looked bad, as far as our getting back together. She had her own store, making costume clothing. Rick was really into sports and had lettered in his freshman year in high school. Debbie was assistant manager in a K-Bee toy store in Atlanta, and had a beautiful apartment.

It was now the last of May, 1982. Stan and I planned a trip to Georgia to see his brother and sister. Of course, I was praying for a miracle . . . hoping to see and talk to Miko.

Phoning Miko, I told her we were coming up to see them in about three weeks and asked her for a date. "Let me take you to church, please."

Miko laughed, but said, "Okay. I guess we can't get into much trouble there."

Not only did we go to church, but we spent a lot of time together that week, getting to know each other again. We stayed at Debbie's apartment. Miko and Rick, who lived in a trailer, came and spent most of the week with us. The sweetest memories from that week were our first family devotions. God was there with us, and we knew it.

Stan, Rick, and Debbie. It was a wonderful weekend.

CHAPTER ELEVEN

Miracles Still Happen

My father and mother, having been down from Alaska on vacation, had stopped by to see Miko and the children two weeks earlier. They were anxiously waiting and praying to see what was going to happen.

Though many details had to be taken care of, God had everything worked out. Rick came back to Florida with Stan and me, and we started getting a plan ready for the family.

Debbie did not want to leave her job and nice apartment. Her mother wouldn't come to Florida without her. We kept on praying, and God kept working. Then Debbie had an accident at work that caused her to be flat on her back for a while. God spoke to her and told her to move to Florida. Two long years and four months of separation had ended.

Our first day back together

I thank the good Lord for His great loving mercy; He saw fit not only to bring my family back together again, but to do it while my father and mother (who had faithfully prayed for us for many years) were there to witness this happy and glorious occasion.

As in any large construction site, there were occasional nude pictures of women around the plant. One lunchroom, in particular, was covered with nudes. It had been that way for years. I didn't have to go there, so I simply avoided it.

There was another building, however, which I was required to go in once a week for safety meetings. Much to my dismay, the place was covered, literally wallpapered, with graphic pornography! The men, at least most of them, seemed to be pleased with the newly decorated walls . . . especially the man who had just finished putting them up. Tattoo was what they called him, for obvious reasons. I don't think he had more than a square inch on his entire body that wasn't tattooed. Tattoo was more than glad to show or describe to anyone the ones that weren't visible.

I asked my family and the church to start praying about it. Then God said something to me I really didn't want to hear. He said, "Tell the man that put those pictures up that you are praying about it, and that I'm going to take them down."

"God," I asked, "are You sure? What if it's not really You?"

Again I talked to my family about it, saying, "This is really important. What if I tell him that, and the pictures don't come down? Then it's going to make me look stupid, and it'll make God look bad."

Rick said, "Dad, if it's God telling you to do this, you don't have to worry about how it makes anyone look."

Then, Debbie added, "Not only am I going to pray, that the pictures come down, I'm going to pray that the person who put them up is the one who takes them down."

The next day I prayed all the way to work, "God, if this is You, and You're really going to take those pictures down, then make it clear. Give me the opportunity to talk to Tattoo this morning."

This was asking a lot, as there were over two thousand men employed at the plant, and he worked with a different crew. When I entered the building where I worked, there he was, all by himself.

I said, "Okay, Lord. You're gonna have to help me."

"Sam," I said, calling him by his real name, "I want to talk to you about all those pictures."

"What about 'em?" he snapped.

"I just want to let you know that God is going to take them down. I am praying for God to take down all those filthy pictures, and He is going to do it."

Sam blew his top and started shouting, "Everyone likes those pictures but you! It's none of your business. What right do you have to interfere? You're the only one who doesn't like 'em."

It had started out being just the two of us, but by now he had attracted a crowd.

"Sam," I said, "you didn't hear what I said. I didn't say I was going to management and complain. I didn't say I was going to your supervisor and complain. I said . . . I'm talking to God about it, and God is going to take down all those pictures."

He just stood there looking bewildered, then walked off muttering to himself.

Feeling fantastic and full of faith, there was no more doubt in my mind that those pictures were coming down. I'd tell it to anyone who'd listen. The word was out, and the men were talking about it. I brought everyone at church up to date on what had transpired and asked them to pray.

Entering the building each morning, on the way to my work area, it was necessary to go through a hallway. Halfway down this hallway, on one side was an open doorway that led directly to the building which had all the dirty pictures in it. Looking out this doorway and through a window into that building, I could see if the pictures were still on the wall.

The first day after I had told Sam the pictures were coming down, I entered the hallway, stopped, and looked through the window. The pictures were still there. The second day, I entered the hallway, stopped, and looked through the window. The pictures were still there. The third day, I entered the hallway, stopped, and looked through the window, but I couldn't see any pictures. Already rejoicing, I walked quickly over to the building and entered the doorway. In the middle of the room were three large trash cans filled to capacity. There was Tattoo, stuffing the last few pictures into the trash.

All eyes were on me as I stood in that doorway. I let out a big "Praise the Lord!"

I will never forget the looks on their faces. Tattoo was as mad as a junkyard dog, but everyone else was smiling . . . with a look of amazement.

One man from Jamaica started saying, "Vern prayed 'em down! Vern prayed 'em down!" The site superintendent had given orders for the pictures to be taken down immediately by whoever had put them up.

I thank God, over and over, for the miraculous way He has changed the lives of my family and me. I had done everything as wrong as it possibly could have been done. I'd cursed God, was unfaithful to my wife, taught my children God didn't exist, lived deep in sin, did my best to kill myself with drugs, and put my dear wife and precious children through a living hell over and over again. When God rescued me, He had to reach down a long way.

Epilogue

In 1983, two years after I got saved, my mother passed away. On her last day, she told how God richly blessed her soul. Though the doctor told her about the seriousness of her condition, she could hardly sleep that night because she was so thrilled about going to heaven.

Mom told the young girl that was her hospital roommate, "I'm going to the Glory Land!"

"Glory Land? Where's that?" she asked.

"Heaven," Mom replied. "Haven't you heard?"

A few hours later Mom left this earth to be with God forever.

In 1984, Miko and I helped open the Victory Children's Home in Fort Pierce, Florida. We acquired a building that was formerly the youth detention center. With the help of a lot of volunteers, we cleaned it up, removed all the barbed wire, took the bars off the windows, applied a lot of paint, and turned it into a home for abused and abandoned children. We were there for two years. The home is still operating and has since moved to Port St. Lucie.

In 1999, Miko and I flew to Alaska to attend my father's funeral. He had married a wonderful woman, who made the last years of his life some of the best. I'm sure Mom was there to welcome him home.

This is the second printing of this book, *Hope for the Hopeless*. As of this year, 2007, I have not had nor do I have any desire to do drugs since I got saved in 1980. However, pornography has become another issue. I believe that every Christian has at least one weakness in his life: an Achilles heel, if you will. Mine happens to be pornography. It is an area in my life that I thought was settled long ago, yet it has come back to haunt me more times than I care to admit. **Satan knows our weaknesses, and he will never leave us alone. If through Christ, we gain one victory over him, he will try doubly hard to regain control of our life in some other way. Beware!**

I spend long hours on the computer doing God's work, reaching around the world with the good news of Christ through www.SomebodyCares4U.com. On the other side of the good news is a barrage of temptation ranging from soft porn to hard core and beyond. All this is readily available in the privacy of my own home with the click of a few keys on my computer. I found myself spending more and more time looking at porn and I knew that once again, I had a major problem.

I was there for a lot longer than I care to admit, but I did something about it. I got sick and tired of sneaking around, fearing, and dreading the next time I'd be caught, and knowing how it was breaking my wife's heart every time I tried to lie my way out of it.

I cried out to God for help and kept crying for help, knowing I couldn't break the chains of addiction to Internet Porn by myself. One day I went on the Internet and typed in "ADDICTION TO PORNOGRAPHY," and was led to a site called "SETTING CAPTIVES FREE" and ordered the course. Faithfully reading the daily lessons in this course helped me understand the Biblical principles in dealing with addictions.

I then did one of the most difficult things I've ever done. I made an appointment with my pastor whom I'd known for many years. He was a man who believed in me and for years had supported this very ministry as we reach out to help others in need.

I confessed to him that I had been living a lie and asked for his forgiveness. He prayed. I prayed. I cried my heart out to God asking His forgiveness and for His Grace, which would give me the desire and also the power to do His will. I then went home and confessed to my wife how I had been unfaithful to her every time I viewed porn on the Internet, and pled for her forgiveness. I asked her to help me be accountable for my actions and to question me daily in a loving spirit. She agreed, and I agreed that I would be honest with her, no matter what.

Friends, let me tell you: something wonderful has happened! The chains of bondage have been broken. God has set me free. What was formerly such a powerful magnet has become repulsive to me. My personal relationship with Christ has been restored, and I have a peace in my heart that passes all understanding. To God be the glory!

I do not confess this wretched sin in my life because I was caught and am now making an attempt to wriggle my way out of a bad situation. I tell you this to let you know that **God was faithful to me to continually convict me of sin.** I am also telling you this because I know that there are thousands of people, including ministers, who have been snared by this insidious evil so readily available through the Internet. Pornography will destroy Christianity like a cancer if we don't stop and admit that there's a monster in our homes that is no longer a dirty little secret we can hide under the mattress.

If you are one of the thousands that has been caught up in this evil trap, whatever your position, please, please make the decision to stop trying to quit by yourself. It can't be done. Take the necessary steps to a full recovery that only God can give. You've got to start someplace. If you don't talk to someone, it will remain your dirty little secret, **and Satan will continue to control your life.**

http:/www.settingcaptivesfree.com/home/

This is a quote by the late Adrian Rogers:

> SIN will take you farther than you ever wanted to go,
> keep you longer than you ever wanted to stay,
> and cost you more than you ever expected to pay."

The End

www.SomebodyCares4U.com